THE
Revelation
OF
Ruth

CANDACE N. FORD

LOVE CLONES
publishing

Love Clones Publishing
www.lcpublishing.net

Printed in the United States of America

First Printing, 2014

ISBN: 978-0692296158

Publishers:
Love Clones Publishing
Dallas, TX
www.lcpublishing.net

DEDICATION

The Revelation of Ruth is dedicated to the
beautiful, talented, anointed, gifted, single woman
who is patiently waiting for God to reveal you to
your Boaz. May the Lord continue to bless, protect
and cover you in your waiting season.

ACKNOWLEDGMENTS

I would like to acknowledge the twenty-six single, saved and satisfied women who enrolled in the first Revelation of Ruth teleconference class in May of 2014. I thank you for trusting me to be used by the Holy Spirit, to teach and train you all to be prepared to be revealed by God. I look forward to seeing those beautiful wedding invitations in the mail!

Contents

Introduction -6

Chapter 1
The Fact of the Matter -17

Chapter 2
A Man and His Land -28

Chapter 3
I Will Do Whatever You Say-47

Chapter 4
Will He Assume The Responsibility of You -63

Chapter 5
Conclusion -77

Introduction

Ruth 1:16 – 17 (GW) But Ruth answered, "Don't force me to leave you. Don't make me turn back from following you. Wherever you go, I will go, and wherever you stay, I will stay. Your people will be my people, and your God will be my God. Wherever you die, I will die, and I will be buried there with you. May the Lord strike me down if anything but death separates you and me!"

The story of Ruth and Boaz is an account that every Christian is familiar with and is taught to assist single women who are waiting to be married. This is a sad story, a riveting story, and a love story, told in four chapters in the book of Ruth. In my teachings to single women I have often used this story to explain how to be found by a man of God, how to submit to womanly wisdom, and how to be where you're supposed to be in order to be discovered by your "Boaz".

Reading through the chapters of the Book of Ruth makes the "dating-game" seem so simple and seemingly effortless, but the real world is definitely not that way. Women are waiting but have no revelation of "the wait". Men are looking but have no revelation of "the seek". Divorcees are thinking that they will never be found; widows believe their marriage life is dead, and widowers would prefer not to "try" marriage again. No matter why people are single, they are, and many are single in the dark because revelation is needed to bring light on how to walk with God, wait on God, trust God, and seek God while believing for a mate.

Paul prayed for the church of Ephesus to obtain wisdom and revelation from the Holy Spirit in order to know Christ better and to have deeper insight.

Ephesians 1:17-20 (GW) reads: I pray that the glorious Father, the God of our Lord Jesus Christ, would give you a spirit of wisdom and revelation as you come to know Christ better. [18] Then you will have deeper insight. You will know the confidence that he calls you to have and the glorious wealth that God's people will inherit. [19] You will also know the unlimited greatness of his power as it works with might and strength for us, the believers. [20] He worked with that same power in Christ when he brought him back to life and gave him the highest position in heaven.

As Christians we need wisdom in general to walk upright before the Lord, but we also need wisdom and revelation in specific areas of our lives. We need revelation when dealing with our finances, our children, our jobs and especially our marital status.

So what is revelation? Revelation is defined as something revealed or disclosed, especially a striking disclosure, as of something not before realized. Synonyms of revelation are announcement, discovery, epiphany, prophecy, proclamation, eye-opener, uncover, unveiling, and manifestation. In the word of God you see revelation as God's disclosure of Himself and His will to His people. Revelation is how God show us who He is on a collective and an individual basis. For instance, where I may need God to reveal Himself to me as a provider, another person may need Him to reveal Himself as a friend. God will meet us wherever we need Him in whichever area we yield ourselves to Him, because He is so awesome.

Single ladies, if you want God to reveal Himself to you as a friend, a provider, a confidant, a father, or a keeper, you must yield your singleness to Him. As a result of your yielding, God can then reveal you to your future spouse! Besides, it is God who must do the revealing. God wants to keep you under the "cloak of singleness" to process you. Under this cloak, He shows you love, He gives you wisdom and understanding of who He has called you to be, He shows you how beautiful you are, how precious you are and how important it is for you to be whole as a single woman so that you may be whole as a married woman. You must stay under this cloak until God deems you ready for marriage and you should never rob Him of His responsibility to unveil you to your spouse.

As you read this book it will shine light on how awesome the experience of being single in God is. It will demolition the many lies the enemy has whispered in your ear that you are worthless, unloved, unproductive or unattractive. It will dispel the enemy's lies that you will never get married again because your first marriage didn't work or because your spouse died and you now have to live a life alone.

While reading through The Revelation of Ruth, allow the Holy Spirit to minister to you about where you are and where you need to be in preparation for marriage. Please allow God to reveal to you who He has called you to be and how important it is for you to fall in love with Him as He orders your steps to be found.

Let's Go!

ARE YOU READY FOR GOD TO REVEAL YOU IN DUE SEASON?

I have mentored many single women and the first statement that I generally hear is "I'm ready to get married." However, my response to them is, have you revealed everything to God in order for Him to reveal you? Most times single women are so ready to marry that they believe they are ready to BE married. They see themselves walking down the aisle in their beautiful dress; their family is present, a myriad of flowers, gifts and bridesmaids. Yet they never stop to think about letting go of the un-forgiveness to which they are holding from hurts of past relationships. They never stop to think about the things that God has ordained for them to accomplish as a single woman before they get married. They never stop to think about being prepared to submit to a husband because they have had submission issues in other relationships.

Women, in your singleness you have to keep all lines of communication open with God. You must be open with him about your hurts, your fears, your doubts, your likes and your dislikes. In the single season of your life you should learn how to be an open book with God because you will have to be an open book with your husband. The oldest trick of the enemy is to get you in a position of hiding through disobedience or holding on to anything opposite of God. The first sin in the bible was disobedience that resulted in Adam hiding.

Genesis 3:8-11 (NIV): Then the man and his wife heard the sound of the Lord God as he was walking in the garden in the cool of the day, and they hid from the Lord God among the trees of the garden. But the Lord God called to the man, "Where are you?" He answered, "I heard you in the garden, and I was afraid because I was naked; so I hid." And he said, "Who told you that you were naked? Have you eaten from the tree that I commanded you not to eat from?"

After Adam had sinned, he was deceived into hiding himself from God. His shame, personal disappointment or fear caused him to try to run away from the presence of the Lord. He tried to hide from God's light instead of running to it, instead of revealing his mistake, his hurt or his confusion. You cannot allow the enemy to isolate you in your singleness. You cannot allow the enemy to lie to you. Fill in the blank with your name and ask yourself, "_____ where are you?"

Have you been open with God about your sin, your doubt, or your offenses? Are you ready to reveal these things to God at His throne in order to obtain the healing that you need to be whole before marriage is even put on the table?

The Psalmist put it plainly in Ps. 138:8-9: "Where can I go to get away from your Spirit? Where can I run to get away from you? If I go up to heaven, you are there. If I make my bed in hell, you are there." God will not reveal you to your husband if you are not willing to stop running and start being honest, knowing that you cannot hide from God. You must give the Lord the secret things of your heart. You cannot be afraid of God's healing power because it is needed to clean you of anything that would keep you back from having a fruitful, Kingdom advancing marriage. It is your revealing of these things that will then cause God to reveal you in due season to the one man who will love you like Christ loves the Church.

In your single season the one thing that you must keep in the forefront of your mind is that God loves you. He wants the best for you and He is willing to keep you hidden in Him until the man He has for you is ready, spiritually, emotionally, socially and financially, to properly cover you. There is no need to rush the revealing process because while you are hidden under God's wings He is preparing you. Finally, your disclosure is contingent on you being obedient to God, submitting to wisdom, and you undoubtedly knowing who God has called you to be.

I recall, a few years before my husband found me, I was in a terrible relationship with someone I desired to be my husband, not because he could be, but because I wanted to be married. I wanted a husband, I wanted a family, and my self-esteem was so low I was willing to settle for a "piece of a man" to fulfill this desire. I wasn't willing to allow God to keep me hidden; I was going to make it happen on my own.

Trust me, ordering my own steps caused me much pain. It caused me to hide from God instead of running to Him. Yet God in His mercy and love beckoned me to come back under His cloak of preparation. He called my name, forgave me and hid me in Him once again to protect me from counterfeits until He deemed it time for me to be found.

If you are truly ready to be married, you must wait for God to do the revealing! Do not run from under the cloak prematurely; allow God to remove it in due season. Furthermore, don't allow the enemy to tell you in this waiting season that you must run and get married to satisfy your physical desires. The same power of the Holy Spirit that raised Jesus from the dead can keep you from masturbating, can keep you from fornicating, and can keep you from being the "side-chick." It can keep you from finding yourself in relationships in which you shouldn't be! Shacking is not a substitute for marriage. He is not to going to leave his wife, and if he does, he will cheat on you just like he cheated on her.

In this time of your life you should be focused on getting *you* right, discovering your purpose, learning balance between work and life, and understanding how to spend intimate times with Christ. Before Eve, Adam worked very closely with

God. He named the animals, worked in the garden, and it was just him and God. Do you spend time studying the word of God? Do you spend time in prayer for you and for others? Are you being obedient to God in regards to starting a business, birthing a ministry or publishing a book? You know you, and God wants to reveal you *whole* because a true man of God does not want half of a woman.

When God reveals you this will ensure you being properly unveiled to your future husband, the spiritual cloak will be pulled off and reveal his good thing in you! Besides you will be a good thing because you have allowed God to process you. Consider, you can't skip the "single-season processing" because your body is getting hot, or because your girlfriends are getting married, and because you keep asking God, "When will it be my turn?" You want your turn to be when God is ready to reveal you. Your husband will then find you just as Boaz found Ruth.

Proverbs 29:18 (MSG): If people can't see what God is doing, they stumble all over themselves; But when they attend to what he reveals, they are most blessed.

Let's go further into the process of being revealed.

CHAPTER 1

The Fact of
the Matter

Daniel 2:22 (AMP): "He reveals the deep and secret things; He knows what is in the darkness, and the light dwells with Him."

Generally, when we study the word of God, we simply read the chapters verse by verse without delving into the context and history related to the scripture passage. This way of study gives us a skewed view or interpretation of what we are reading. That is why we must ask the Holy Spirit to give us insight and revelation on the purpose of the passage and how it can be applied to our current situation.

Ruth is not the only single woman in the bible who was prepared or "set-up" for marriage. Esther as a young girl was chosen to marry the King. Rebecca was found by the servant to marry Isaac. Leah and Rachel were both discovered by Jacob for marriage. Even Mary was espoused to Joseph when God called her to be the mother of Jesus.

There were various accounts in the word of God of single women. As we examine the book of Ruth we must understand who she was and the place and time in which she lived. Again keep in mind our definition of revelation is something revealed or disclosed, especially a striking disclosure, as of something not before realized.

The name Ruth means friend, companion, or beauty. Ruth was not a daughter of Israel; she was in fact a Moabite, the descendants of the incestuous relationship of Lot and his daughter. The Moabites and the Israelites never saw eye to eye, but when a famine hit the city in which Naomi and her family lived, they had no choice but to go to Moab to survive and that is where Naomi's sons found and married Ruth and Orpah.

Ruth 1: 1-5 (GW): In the days when the judges were ruling, there was a famine in the land. A man from Bethlehem in Judah went with his wife and two sons to live for a while in the country of Moab. The man's name was Elimelech, his wife's name was Naomi, and the names of their two sons were Mahlon and Chilion. They were descendants of Ephrathah from Bethlehem in the territory of Judah. They went to the country of Moab and lived there. Now, Naomi's husband Elimelech died, and she was left alone with her two sons. Each son married a woman from Moab. One son married a woman named Orpah, and the other son married a woman named Ruth. They lived there for about ten years. Then both Mahlon and Chilion died as well. So Naomi was left alone, without her two sons or her husband.

Ten years after Naomi and her family came to Moab and married, her sons and her husband died, leaving her alone. Ironically Naomi's name means pleasantness, agreeable, or beauty, but none of these tragedies made her look beautiful, pleasant or agreeable. Names in the Hebrew lifestyle were and are still very important. In your single walk that is why it is very important to "watch" whom you call yourself.

Do you declare you are successful?

Do you declare you are available for God's plans and purposes for your life?

Do you declare you will be a wife?

Do you declare you are a suitable Help?

Who do you say you are?

Paying attention to how you see yourself is imperative in your single season, because "as a man thinks so is he" and you must think of yourself how God thinks of you so that you can happily wait to be revealed.

So Naomi loses her husband and sons and Orpah and Ruth lose their husbands. The most logical thing for Naomi to do was to go back home. She knew she was a foreigner in the Moabite land and with all of her family gone there was no longer a reason to stay.

Ruth 1: 6-10 (GW): Naomi and her daughters-in-law started on the way back from the country of Moab. (While they were still in Moab she heard that the Lord had come to help his people and give them food. So she left the place where she had been living, and her two daughters-in-law went with her.) They began to walk back along the road to the territory of Judah. Then Naomi said to her two daughters-in-law, "Go back! Each of you should go back to your mother's home. May the Lord be as kind to you as you were to me and to our loved ones who have died. May the Lord repay each of you so that you may find security in a home with a husband." When she kissed them goodbye, they began to cry loudly. They said to her, "We are going back with you to your people."

Close your eyes and imagine this scene. Three women, one older standing in the position of the matriarch and two young women standing in the middle of the road disheartened, crying, angry, bitter, and full of sorrow. Naomi had no husband, and Ruth and Orpah had no husbands or any children to raise in honor of their deceased husbands. They stood in the middle of the road with nothing, no earthly covering, and no husband to support them, and no expectant future, only a gloomy present.

Have you ever felt that way in your singleness, where it seems as though nothing is working? Every man you think is your husband ends up causing you pain and causing a little piece of you to die. Every time you end up in these dead-end relationships, where you have given yourself physically, emotionally, financially and spiritually and receive nothing in return but excuses and lack of support. You discover yourself standing in the middle of your purpose road crying and totally unsure of the future. Well this was the same position that these three women found themselves in as their souls cried for each other collectively and for themselves individually. The only thing that they could think of was to go back to the people of their husbands as Naomi had heard that the Lord had restored her hometown and the famine was over.

THE LAWS OF THE LAND

Ruth 1:8-13 (GW) Then Naomi said to her two daughters-in-law, "Go back! Each of you should go back to your mother's home. May the Lord be as kind to you as you were to me and to our loved ones who have died. May the Lord repay each of you so that you may find security in a home with a husband." When she kissed them goodbye, they began to cry loudly. They said to her, "We are going back with you to your people." But Naomi said, "Go back, my daughters. Why should you go with me? Do I have any more sons in my womb who could be your husbands? Go back, my daughters. Go, because I am too old to get married again. If I said that I still have hope. . . . And if I had a husband tonight. . . . And even if I gave birth to sons, would you wait until they grew up and stay single just for them? No, my daughters. My bitterness is much worse than yours because the Lord has sent me so much trouble."

Naomi loved her daughters, but she knew she could not physically give them another set of husbands. All of her steps and actions were in regards to the law of the land and how she was taught. According to the law given to Moses from God to the children of Israel, when a man died, his brother was to marry his wife and take care of her, but there were no more sons and she was too old to have any more, and besides her husband was dead as well.

Deuteronomy 25:5 explains the circumstances according to the law as: *"the brother of a man who died without children has an obligation to marry the widow."* Yep everything about Naomi's life seemed bleak and she could not assist her daughters-in-law. So she instructed them to go back, not being cruel, but being realistic.

The life of a single individual is most of the time filled with the questions of why and when: "Why am I not married yet?" and "When will I be found?" With Naomi's sons dead, she knew that her daughters would ask her these questions and she would have no answers, but Ruth didn't care about those questions. All she wanted was for her mother-in-law to grant her wish and not leave her.

Ruth 1:14-18 (GW) They began to cry loudly again. Then Orpah kissed her mother-in-law goodbye, but Ruth held on to her tightly. Naomi said, "Look, your sister-in-law has gone back to her people and to her gods. Go back with your sister-in-law." But Ruth answered, "Don't force me to leave you. Don't make me turn back from following you. Wherever you go, I will go, and wherever you stay, I will stay. Your people will be my people, and your God will be my God. Wherever you die, I will die, and I will be buried there with you. May the Lord strike me down if anything but death separates you and me!" When Naomi saw that Ruth was determined to go with her, she ended the conversation.

Your single walk with God has to be determined! You must make the determination that you are going to follow God, follow who God has instructed you to follow and follow wisdom in order to be properly prepared and thus properly revealed. Many singles give up when it seems as if God is taking too long or when they fall into an unbearable situation. However, God is in it for the long haul and you should be too! God is ready to make your life as a single fulfilling and purposeful, and before you are revealed you must make it a point to connect with wise women who have nothing to give you but their God!

TIMING IS EVERYTHING WITH GOD

Ruth 1:19-22: So both of them went on until they came to Bethlehem. When they entered Bethlehem, the whole town was excited about them. "This can't be Naomi, can it?" the women asked. She answered them, "Don't call me Naomi [Sweet]. Call me Mara [Bitter] because the Almighty has made my life very bitter. I went away full, but the Lord has brought me back empty. Why do you call me Naomi when the Lord has tormented me and the Almighty has done evil to me?" When Naomi came back from the country of Moab, Ruth, her Moabite daughter-in-law, came along with her. They happened to enter Bethlehem just when the barley harvest began.

Naomi and Ruth journeyed back to Bethlehem because Naomi's family was of the tribe of Judah. All Naomi knew to do was to go back to what was familiar to her and Ruth was okay following her because she vowed to go with her wherever she went. Ruth didn't know what was before her, but she was sure she didn't want what was behind her.

In verse 22, it reads, "They happened to enter Bethlehem just when the barley harvest began." You must see God's hand in all of this—the timing, the place and the people involved. Although God doesn't operate in time, He will use it to bring His plans to pass. You being found by your husband is definitely not a surprise to God. It may be a surprise to you or even to your future husband, but God is strategic, He is well aware of the time, place and what position you need to be in to be revealed to your future spouse. Yet you will only be found walking with God and walking with the assistance He has designated to you in your season of singleness.

We will see as we read on, how important it was that Ruth and Naomi returned in the time of harvest, and you as a single woman must be in time and on time to be found. You cannot be operating on your own agenda if you are ready to be found by your husband. You must yield to the Holy Ghost! The Holy Ghost will keep you in timing of God's heartbeat towards you and allow you to be productive in your singleness. Walking with God and not rushing before Him or lagging behind Him will allow your preparation period in singleness to be purposeful and ordained by God.

CHAPTER 2

A Man and His Land

Ruth 2:1-3 (GW): Naomi had a relative. He was from Elimelech's side of the family. He was a man of outstanding character named Boaz. Ruth, who was from Moab, said to Naomi, "Please let me go to the field of anyone who will be kind to me. There I will gather the grain left behind by the reapers." Naomi told her, "Go, my daughter." So Ruth went. She entered a field and gathered the grain left behind by the reapers. Now it happened that she ended up in the part of the field that belonged to Boaz, who was from Elimelech's family.

WHO WAS BOAZ?

The name Boaz translated means, "by strength." He was a wealthy landowner, and the bible says Boaz was a man of outstanding character. He was prominent, respected, and a man of worth. Boaz was a relative of Naomi and her deceased husband, Elimelech. Boaz was a mighty man of wealth. This wealth was evident because he was a landowner, and land is an asset that never depreciates or loses its value. Boaz was a man of character. He wasn't a *character*; He had substance. He was a man whose business had persevered through a famine. He was the type of man that a Godly woman should desire as a husband. A man who could go through the fire and not smell like smoke; a man who when times got rough, he wouldn't go off crying like a little girl but who would continue to walk in integrity and handle the affairs of his business. He was a man of substance!

I truly believe that Boaz was not a loner. He had friends, maybe not many, but some. He was not a recluse. Single ladies, be very concerned when you are courting a man and they have no aspirations, they don't know how to speak or communicate or hold a decent conversation. Yes, he may look like Denzel, but what good is it to be on Denzel's arm and he is anti-social or does not know how to conduct himself in public? A Kingdom husband should be a man who understands that he has a future, a man with vision and one who can communicate that vision to you.

God made Eve to be a suitable helper for Adam. However, Eve had to be aware of what Adam needed help doing in order to help him! God had given Adam a charge to have dominion, be fruitful and multiply; that was his life's purpose, his future and heaven's mandate for his life. Eve was to assist him in getting this accomplished. You cannot be interested in marrying a person who does not know what they were put on this earth to do. He may not know all of the ins and outs, but he must know the vision God has for his life in order for you to be a proper helper.

That's why in your courting season, just because he says he "found you," you cannot lose your mind and stop discerning. When you date a man, you can ask him about his profession and his hobbies, but remember those things are temporal. He could lose his job tomorrow and change his hobbies as well. Those are secondary questions. Your first question should be "What is the vision for your life?" If he says "What is vision?" you should hurry and ask the waiter for the check! You don't want to go down the road of wasting your time with someone who has not spent time with God to get his heavenly directives for his life.

Ladies, you should desire a husband who can see spiritually, who can hear from God, who has aspirations and vision for something other then getting you in bed. God revealed Ruth to a man of substance, a man of character, a man who was respected and valued vision.

My husband had always lived in the home with his mother and his grandmother in Chicago, IL, except when he attended Oral Roberts University in Tulsa, OK for his college education. His mom is an only child and so is he. So they've always been very close. Many single women may have turned their nose up not wanting to marry a man who lived with his mother, but in whatever "state" or position he is in when he finds you, you will be able to predict how his interaction will be with you by the way he interacts with those closes to him.

I observed my husband honor his mother, assist with the finances of the home, attend to her natural needs in regards to doctor's visits, grocery shopping, and taking her to the beauty salon. I observed his love in action for her and never once did I think him a "mama's boy," but I saw a strong man honoring his mother and his genuine concern for her well-being.

When your potential husband comes on the scene watch his interactions with others. Does he have children from a previous relationship for whom he does not provide? He isn't the one. Why? Because I Timothy 5:8 (GW) clearly states, If anyone doesn't take care of his own relatives, especially his immediate family, he has denied the

Christian faith and is worse than an unbeliever. Are you prepared to marry someone who is worse than an unbeliever?

When your potential husband comes on the scene and you observe that he is verbally abusive to those around him, he isn't the one. Why? Because Ecclesiastes 7:9 (GW) declares, Don't be quick to get angry, because anger is typical of fools. Are you ready to marry a fool?

When your potential husband comes on the scene and it seems that he always owes someone money, but never pays, he isn't the one. Why? Because Romans 13:9 (a) says, Pay your debts as they come due. Are you ready to marry a man who doesn't adhere to the word of the Lord?

As I observed my husband with his mother, I fell in love with him more. I knew that if I accepted him as my Boaz, that he would in turn love me with that same compassion, even at a greater level through our covenant relationship. I also understood that the blessing of the Lord rested upon my husband because he honored his mother, and who would not want to marry a blessed man?

Ladies, how he treats those around him, is how he will treat you. So observe, stay alert, pray and be honest with yourself when you see unbecoming tendencies in him. When you are found, your future husband should be a man of character, honesty, integrity and love. That's who you want to be revealed to!

WISDOM IS KEY

As Ruth entered into covenant with Naomi when she declared "and your God will be my God." She also submitted to Naomi's wisdom and direction. Many times in our single, independent lives, we get so dependent on ourselves that we get the "know it all" syndrome. This is another way for the enemy to isolate you. It's a way to make you believe that no one can assist you or that you are capable of "learning" on your own, and this is far from the truth.

In your season of singleness, God wants you to be surrounded and submitted to wise counsel. This is the time of your life for you to join the submission boot camp, for if you can submit to a spiritual Naomi in your singleness, you can submit to your husband in your marriage. Ruth submitted to Naomi because she was in an unfamiliar place, physically and spiritually. She could no longer ask her husband what to do because he was deceased.

She didn't know where to find work in order that she and Naomi could eat because she had never lived in Bethlehem. This unfamiliar place dictated a need for her to seek Naomi for direction and she wasn't ashamed to ask. Don't be too proud to get assistance in your singleness, but make sure that assistance is wise and not from fools.

Consequently, Naomi releases her to go to work and as she works she finds herself in Boaz's land. She finds herself in his area of influence. Many times the Lord will lead us away from what is familiar to us in order to be found. Therefore, if you are willing to submit to wise counsel and the leading of the Holy Spirit, your feet will find themselves in a place to be revealed to your future husband. This place may not be customary to you, but that is the point. You want to be found in a place that is customary to your Boaz, because that is the place in which you will assist him the greatest.

When my husband found me, he found me at the altar during my ordination into the function of an Elder. He was a full-time pastor who was asked by an Apostle to assist in the services. I didn't know him. He didn't know me. However, because ordinations, church services and such were a place of familiarity to him he accepted the invitation to assist. My husband so eloquently tells the story that as I came to kneel at the altar to have hands laid on me for ministry, a bright light covered me and he knew within his spirit man that I was his wife. Did he run up to me after the service and tell me what he saw? No. He prayed, he sought the Lord and as we courted and began to learn one another, God showed us both why He was bringing us together in marriage. One reason only, to advance the Kingdom of God in ministry, family and business.

Being properly revealed is truly based on your obedience to God, your submission to spiritual leadership, and many times your willingness to step outside of your comfort zone. 99.9 percent of the time your Boaz is not going to be the UPS man showing up to your doorstep to deliver a package. Although it has happened, it's generally not the norm. You are going to have to get out of your housecoat and slippers and be about your purpose, working the field for God, doing what He has called you to do so that he can order your steps for revelation.

WHAT ARE YOU PORTRAYING TO YOUR POTENTIAL SPOUSE?

Ruth 2:4-7 (GW): Just then, Boaz was coming from Bethlehem, and he said to his reapers, "May the Lord be with all of you!" They answered him, "May the Lord bless you!" Boaz asked the young man in charge of his reapers, "Who is this young woman?" The young man answered, "She's a young Moabite woman who came back with Naomi from the country of Moab. She said, 'Please let me gather grain. I will only gather among the bundles behind the reapers.' So she came here and has been on her feet from daybreak until now. She just sat down this minute in the shelter."

Single ladies, no man of God wants to marry a lazy woman. Point blank. Determination is attractive to a man with vision. Visionaries are attracted to hard-workers and other visionaries. They are attracted to a Woman of Purpose.

As Boaz returned to his land to greet his workers, his eyes immediately went to someone with whom he was not familiar. He knew all of his employees. Remember, we said he was a man of integrity and man who handled the affairs of his business, so he was well aware of whom his workers were. However, she did not just catch his eye because of her outer beauty, but because of her work ethic. He was attracted to her ability to work on a land reaping, knowing that her only pay was what she gathered behind the paid reapers. His manager told him, "She has been on her feet from daybreak until now." That was fascinating to Boaz and he wanted to know more about this woman!

What are you portraying to your potential spouse? What are you doing with the gifts God has placed in you? You may not be "lazy." You may go to work everyday but what do you do to advance the Kingdom of God? It is important to know that what you do to advance the Kingdom as a single individual, as God has directed you, will align you with what God has told your future husband to do, so when you come together it will truly be a match made in heaven.

There was something about Ruth's beauty shown through her working that attracted Boaz. By working for nothing her actions spoke louder than words. They said, "I may not be able to work in the field like the employees but I'm going to work. So I will pick up the left overs of the employees, because I have to provide for my family. I am grateful that I was not left alone, that Naomi did not leave me, and I will do my part to take care of her." What good man would not be attracted to this type of woman? The bible is clear that "He who finds a wife finds a good thing and obtains favor from the Lord" (Proverbs 18:22). But let me assure you, you must first be that "good thing" as a single woman, and when you become his wife, the good that you have done in obedience, faith, love, patience, and work unto the Lord, will set your husband up nicely to be favored by God.

THE ATTRACTED APPROACHES THE ATTRACTOR

Ruth 2:8-16 (GW): Boaz said to Ruth, "Listen, my daughter. Don't go in any other field to gather grain, and don't even leave this one. Stay here with my young women. Watch where my men are reaping, and follow the young women in that field. I have ordered my young men not to touch you. When you're thirsty, go to the jars and drink some of the water that the young men have drawn." Ruth immediately bowed down to the ground and said to him, "Why are you so helpful? Why are you paying attention to me? I'm only a foreigner." Boaz answered her, "People have told me about everything you have done for your mother-in-law after your husband died. They told me how you left your father and mother and the country where you were born. They also told me how you came to people that you didn't know before. May the Lord reward you for what you have done! May you receive a rich reward from the Lord God of Israel, under whose protection you have come for shelter." Ruth replied, "Sir, may your kindness to me continue. You have comforted me and reassured me, and I'm not even one of your own servants." When it was time to eat, Boaz told her, "Come here. Have some bread, and dip it into the sour wine." So she sat beside the reapers, and he handed her some roasted grain. She ate all she wanted and had some left over. When she got up to gather grain, Boaz ordered his servants, "Let her gather grain even among the bundles. Don't give her any problems. Even pull some grain out of the bundles and leave it for her to gather. Don't give her a hard time about it."

God is a God of order and once He does something in the earth, it becomes a precedent. Eve was brought to Adam, not Adam to Eve. This was the first union in the history of man, and the way it was done in the Garden, God expected it to be done on the farm, in the city, on the mountain and in the valley!

As the love story continues, Boaz approached Ruth. He inquired of her identity to the manager. But this secondhand information was not enough; he approached her.

Let me interject here: Ladies, if you have been dating a man for more than twenty-four months and he has not approached the subject of marriage, he may not be the one for you.

Okay back to Ruth...

Boaz was legitimately concerned with her welfare. He wanted her to know that he was concerned with her safety while she worked. He wanted her to know that he had her best interest at heart as she worked in his field. He also wanted her to know that he knew who she was to his family. Also, did you notice he's asking these questions, not to get her in the bed, but because he was genuinely concerned about her.

Ruth respected his position as the owner of the land. This is a very important factor to take note of. Respect must be present in the introduction, the middle and the end of the dating story, so that it may be ever present in the beginning and duration of your marriage. You cannot marry a man for whom you have no respect. Yes, respect is earned through the process of getting to know one another; however you should never be attracted to a man whom you know you will never respect.

When Boaz approached Ruth she properly bowed down to the ground as an act of reverence of his position. In her bowing she asked why. Unfortunately when we are first revealed to our Boaz we always ask why. Why Lord, why have you given me a man with substance, wealth, and wisdom? Why little *ole* me? God has a man assigned to be your husband who when meeting him will allow you to acknowledge the promise of "exceeding abundantly above all that we ask or think" (Eph. 3:20). Therefore your first thought will be why me Lord. But then you must realize that your coming together with this man is bigger than you and no one but God will get the glory for being the matchmaker who put this union together.

Boaz goes a step further and invites her to his table to eat. Yes, he publicly acknowledges his concern for Ruth. Ladies be aware, if he hides you during courting, he will hide you during your marriage, and an isolated wife is an abused wife.

As well, don't continue or start a relationship with a man who doesn't pay attention when you're talking, a man who cares nothing about what you care about. If he's not interested enough to listen to you when you speak about your goals and aspirations, he won't be interested later when you are married. Everything else will be more important than you, and as a wife you should be the most important person in your husband's life.

Ladies, this chapter of Ruth introduces the man named Boaz. But even in his introduction you can see that his interest in Ruth was not to add her to a harem, make her a slave or even an employee. His intentions were more admirable, more respectable and they were authentic.

STILL SUBMITTED

Ruth 2:17- 23 (GW): So Ruth gathered grain in the field until evening. Then she separated the grain from its husks. She had about half a bushel of barley. She picked it up and went into the town, and her mother-in-law saw what she had gathered. Ruth also took out what she had left over from lunch and gave it to Naomi. Her mother-in-law asked her, "Where did you gather grain today? Just where did you work? May the man who paid attention to you be blessed." So Ruth told her mother-in-law about the person with whom she worked. She said, "The man I worked with today is named Boaz." Naomi said to her daughter-in-law, "May the Lord bless him. The Lord hasn't stopped being kind to people— living or dead." Then Naomi told her, "That man is a relative of ours. He is a close relative, one of those responsible for taking care of us." Ruth, who was from Moab, told her, "He also said to me, 'Stay with my younger workers until they have finished the harvest.'" Naomi told her daughter-in-law Ruth, "It's a good idea, my daughter that you go out to the fields with his young women. If you go to someone else's field, you may be molested." So Ruth stayed with the young women who were working for Boaz. She gathered grain until both the barley harvest and the wheat harvest ended. And she continued to live with her mother-in-law.

I am honored to be a Spiritual Mother to many single women who are waiting for God to reveal them to their future husbands. We have very candid conversations regarding their purpose, their weariness in waiting, their victories, their losses, their times of crying and their times of joy.

We talk about what it means to be a Virtuous Woman, an anointed Help- Meet and what it takes for them to have a successful marriage. I love pouring into them through wisdom and transparency and I love seeing the fruit of my labor, producing women who respect themselves enough to walk in purpose. In your single walk I cannot stress enough about the importance of having a woman or women of wisdom covering you in prayer, encouraging you and speaking into your life as you are in your season of waiting. You may be single but you cannot do this alone!

You need a safe place to run to when your emotions begin to lie to you. You need a safe place to vent when your body begins to lie to you. You need a safe place to run to when you are found and you need to tell someone who will celebrate with you! Naomi was Ruth's safe place and after her encounter with Boaz she came right back to her safe place. She returns home with food and continued to serve.

Ladies, until there is a proposal, a ring and a wedding, your responsibilities prior to being found must remain priority, especially if you are a single mother. This is not the time for you to start neglecting your children's well-being because you have been approached. You are to remain focused in purpose, servant-hood, parenting, and as an employer or an employee. Staying focused is key.

You have to purposely surround yourself with wisdom, connect with someone who will watch out for the wolves. When you start allowing the enemy to isolate you the wolf comes to devour. Moreover, do not surround yourself with silly women! Discern and follow the leading of the Lord as to who should assist you in walking through your single season. A silly woman is not a good candidate to direct you in strolling through the process because when you are revealed to your husband she'll be the first one wanting to steal him from you. So run from the *silly*!

Ruth comes back to her safe place and Naomi confirms Boaz, his instructions to her as to where to glean and gives her further wisdom of how to work and be successful through the entire harvest season. Ruth loved Naomi and Naomi loved Ruth. Therefore their covenant relationship allowed Ruth to be a blessing to Naomi and not a hindrance. It allowed Naomi to have a companion to help ease the pain of losing her husband and her sons. There is safety in covenant!

CHAPTER 3

I Will Do Whatever You Say

Ruth 3:1-5 (GW): Naomi, Ruth's mother-in-law, said to her, "My daughter, shouldn't I try to look for a home that would be good for you? Isn't Boaz, whose young women you've been working with, our relative? He will be separating the barley from its husks on the threshing floor tonight. Freshen up, put on some perfume, dress up, and go down to the threshing floor. Don't let him know that you're there until he's finished eating and drinking. When he lies down, notice the place where he is lying. Then uncover his feet, and lie down there. He will make it clear what you must do." Ruth answered her, "I will do whatever you say."

Proverbs 1:7 (NIV) says, The fear of the Lord is the beginning of knowledge, but fools despise wisdom and instruction. If you are truly ready to step out of your singleness into the life of a married woman, you must have reverence for the Lord and the wisdom, teaching and leading of the Holy Spirit. Many singles are still in the state that they are in because they have no knowledge. They are going about dating whomever, sleeping with whomever, picking up soul-ties like groceries at the store and never stopping to hear or heed to the voice of wisdom.

Proverbs 4:7 (NIV) declares, Wisdom is the principal thing; therefore get wisdom: and with all thy getting get understanding. Our Father never wants us to lack, especially in the area of wisdom, therefore He has given us the Holy Spirit to teach us in all things. Through the Holy Spirit's leading, He will bring us to people, places and things that will give us clear instruction on how to properly serve God while being single, to stay free of foolishness and how to properly be revealed to the man God has for you.

As we enter into Chapter 3 you see the wisdom of the Lord speaking directly to Ruth as words from Naomi, "My daughter, shouldn't I try to look for a home that would be good for you?" Wow! How profound is this question? Naomi is clearly telling Ruth, "It's time for you to be revealed and you will not have to do this alone. I am going to assist you in getting to the place where the man of God can find you and take notice of you, not just for your work in the field but as a prepared woman, ready for marriage."

In your single season you need people in your

life that will not only tell you what time it is but also give you the step-by-step, blow-by-blow instructions of how not to be a girlfriend, but to be a wife. Naomi releases natural wisdom to Ruth. Why? Because no matter how anointed a man is, he is still a man, and men want their five senses to be attracted to you as well as their spirit man. A man wants to embrace your natural beauty. If you recall the story of Esther, the King wanted to give her whatever she asked, not because she was the Queen, but because she was absolutely beautiful. It was her beauty that saved her people not the fact that she could pray in the spirit for five hours or that she could fast for forty days. No, it was her beauty!

Ladies, in this season of your life it is so important to consistently take care of your outward appearance. Although you never want a man to only be attracted to your outer, I would be a liar to suggest that it is not important when the Lord reveals you to your husband. This is definitely the time to get some swag and reassurance about you.

Many women have been bait for the wolves because of insecurities. The wolves, say, "Oh, she doesn't know who she is. Let me take her money, her joy, all of the above. She may have a good job and a good head on her shoulders but her insecurities will cause her to fall for any man." Ladies, spend time getting your womanhood together! You should look nice all the time. Be consistent with your hairdresser, and get your manicure and pedicure scheduled into your calendar. Make sure you own nice pajamas. As a single woman value yourself. Throw out your holey underwear and pajamas from college, which was ten years ago! Have in your possession great smelling perfume, get your face waxed if you have issues with facial hair, handle your personal hygiene, and if you are not pleased with your weight do something to fix it.

SHE FOLLOWED THE INSTRUCTIONS

Ruth 3: 6-10 (GW) Ruth went to the threshing floor and did exactly as her mother-in-law had directed her. Boaz had eaten and drunk to his heart's content, so he went and lay at the edge of a pile of grain. Then she went over to him secretly, uncovered his feet, and lay down. At midnight the man was shivering. When he turned over, he was surprised to see a woman lying at his feet. "Who are you?" he asked. She answered,

"I am Ruth. Spread the corner of your garment over me because you are a close relative who can take care of me." Boaz replied, "May the Lord bless you, my daughter. This last kindness—that you didn't go after the younger men, whether rich or poor—is better than the first.

There is no union without a willingness to obey and submit to the instructions given to you to get to Boaz. I understand that not all of my readers may have a "Naomi" in their life, but that's not an excuse because all my readers do have the HOLY SPIRIT! Therefore, there is a heavenly instructor to show you how to be revealed to your potential husband, but listening, faith and obedience on your part is key.

Naomi gave Ruth very simple instructions she needed to follow in order to properly approach Boaz. The walk to marriage is a two way street. Many single women believe that it's only his responsibility. It is his responsibility to find you, but it's your responsibility to respond to his finding you. You can't expect him to do everything; you play a part and your part is to follow the instructions of the Holy Spirit through your Naomi! I cannot say that when my husband found me that I had one "Naomi," but I did receive great advice from some very wise women. However, where I had no one to tell me what to do, I had to listen to the Lord in regards to the necessary steps to take to walk in integrity, character and wisdom in my courting stage. That is why as a single woman you have to cultivate your relationship with God.

You cannot expect God to send you the answer when you never listen or obey what He tells you to do. Then when you hit the brick wall, you blame God for him leaving you or him getting you pregnant, or you blame God for why you're still single. Well the blame game ends now. You must do whatever God tells you to do. If He tells you to move to another city, get packing. If He tells you to change your church membership, schedule an appointment with your Pastor. If He tells you to forgive, forget, give, sit down, shut up, or move on, you need to do exactly what He says!

Naomi's instruction to Ruth was, freshen up, put on some perfume, dress up, and go down to the threshing floor. Don't let him know that you're there until he's finished eating and drinking. When he lies down, notice the place where he is lying. Then uncover his feet, and lie down there. He will make it clear what you must do." And she followed the instructions to a "T". She trusted Naomi and her actions aligned with that trust.

Do you trust God? Do you know that God wants the best for you when it comes to your spouse? Are you ready to surrender you so that you can enter into holy matrimony? Or are you content living your life by your own rules and missing out on a life of abundance? It's up to you now to make some true personal assessments about where you are in your singleness.

Has God told you to do something and you haven't been obedient? Ruth didn't know what was going to really happen after she followed Naomi's instructions; all she knew was she loved, trusted and was in covenant with Naomi and disobedience is a covenant breaker. She left everything that was familiar to her. For what? A better life and to get that better life she was going to have to listen and heed to wisdom!

After Ruth did exactly what Naomi told her to do, Boaz turned around and simply asked, "Who are you?" Was it dark and Boaz couldn't see who she was. Well my thought is that he asked in surprise, "Who are you? No woman has approached me, being kind, thinking of my well being and wanting nothing in return. No woman has been so tender, kind and attentive to my needs as you." By her act of care and concern, he wanted to then take her hand in marriage. He wanted to take care of her.

Now ladies, her act was not the concern that a child gives a mother, but it was laced with a little seduction. She wanted to be noticed; she wanted him to be aware that she was available. I recall a month before my husband proposed to me, we would talk on the phone, but it just seemed to me that he was beating around the bush. He knew I was his wife and the Lord at this time had revealed it to me as well, but I wanted C. Kevin Ford to tell me himself. I knew exactly what to do to confirm what I already knew. I owned a sharp, cream pant suit, long jacket, high collar, fit curves in all the right places and when I wore it, it turns the heads of men. I knew if I wore this suit, oh and the dark chocolate high-heeled boots with it, in his presence, and it did not evoke a reaction that he was not the one.

I entered his church on a Sunday afternoon and he was preaching. When I walked in, he grabbed the podium and for about sixty seconds lost his train of thought because he saw me walking in, looking good! Yes, women, we can use all of our assets, tastefully, that's why God gave them to us. It's nothing wrong with catching his eye, especially when you are being led by God to be his wife.

THERE SHOULD BE NO FEAR IN COURTING

Ruth 3:11 -13: Don't be afraid, my daughter. I will do whatever you say. The whole town knows that you are a woman who has strength of character. It is true that I am a close relative of yours, but there is a relative closer than I. Stay here tonight. In the morning if he will agree to take care of you, that is good. He can take care of you. But if he does not wish to take care of you, then, I solemnly swear, as the Lord lives, I will take care of you myself. Lie down until morning."

"Perfect love casts out all fear" (1 John 4:18), and you should experience love while courting your Boaz, before you're married and consummate your union. If you don't, you should let that relationship go. Now let me caution you, if you don't know what LOVE is supposed to do, then it's time for you to sit down and spend time with LOVE. I John 4:8 says God is love and I Corinthians 13 explains who LOVE is and what LOVE does.

Love is patient, love is kind. It does not envy, it

does not boast, it is not proud. It does not dishonor others, it is not self-seeking, it is not easily angered, it keeps no record of wrongs. Love does not delight in evil but rejoices with the truth. It always protects, always trusts, always hopes, always perseveres. Love never fails (I Corinthians 13:4-8).

Patience, kindness, humility, honor, are some of the characteristics that you need to see working in your *Potential* and these are characteristics you need to have working in you. Love is an action word and you should be able to see it.

I remember courting my husband and experiencing his love for me in such an awesome way. There were many people, I would even go as far as to say demonic forces, who did their best to keep my husband and I from getting married. Lies, lies and more lies were being released about the both of us and it had come to a point that it was just out of control. People in my husband's church, some of his so-called friends, did not want us to get married because they wanted him all to themselves. They were happy he was single because he was always at their beck and call. It had gotten so bad, that my Boaz said to me, "Babe, I would rather leave you than have you endure this hurt and foolishness."

Of course I was not going to let the enemy steal my man from me, so we endured and came out married, happy and in love! My husband wanting the best for me, even if the best meant him walking away was all I needed to experience to know that he loved me and that when the going got tough, he wouldn't get going! Boaz showed Ruth love and assured her that he would take care of her.

Now let's bring into play the "law of the land" again here because this piece of the pie is very important to the beauty of this love story. Recall in Chapter 1, I introduced the scripture, Deuteronomy 25:5, Remember the circumstances according to the law: 'the brother of a man who died without children has an obligation to marry the widow.'" This law would have definitely applied to Ruth; unfortunately her husband's brother was deceased as well. However, there were other male relatives who could have stood in the dead brother's place so that the "blood-line" would continue.

Boaz tells Ruth, "It is true that I am a close relative of yours, but there is a relative closer than I." Remember, Boaz is a man of character and integrity and he was honest with Ruth, "I love you but I will not break the law to be your husband, there is a relative closer to me." Ladies, this man is trying to keep this woman honest. He doesn't want to sleep with her before marriage and take something that doesn't belong to her. He doesn't ask her to cheat and lie for him and cause a curse to come upon their marriage. He puts the law of God first, even if that means that he could not marry her. This is a man you want God to reveal you to. And you know what? You should wait until he does. Boaz tells Ruth there is another, but if he doesn't do his part, he swears unto the Lord that he will.

When Ruth came back with Naomi, she entered into covenant with her mother-in-law. When Boaz swore to Ruth, he spoke to her in covenant language. These individuals were serious about their relationships with one another. They were interested in keeping their word because they wanted the relationships to work; they knew they needed each other. People in our society don't speak to each other in the language of covenant. We say one thing and do the complete opposite. Some women change beaus like they change their underwear and vice versa. People join a church today and leave in a month. The rate of divorce is higher in the church than it is in the world.

Covenant language is not spoken as often as it should be. However, when you are courting your potential husband you need to enter into covenant with him with regards to your future. You should want to hear him say he will love you like Christ loves the church, that he will love you as he loves his body, that he will provide and cover you as your head. These are covenant words written in the bible that you should want to hear from your potential. If he is still speaking to you superficially about how he's going to rock your world in the bed and that you should be grateful to be with him, you need to drop that jester, because he definitely is not your king.

LET HIM LEAD

Ruth 3:14-18 (GW) So she lay at his feet until morning, but got up before anyone could be recognized; and he said, "No one must know that a woman came to the threshing floor." He also said, "Bring me the shawl you are wearing and hold it out." When she did so, he poured into it six measures of barley and placed the bundle on her. Then he went back to town. When Ruth came to her mother-in-law, Naomi asked, "How did it go,

*my daughter?" Then she told her everything Boaz
had done for her and added, "He gave me these
six measures of barley, saying, 'Don't go back to
your mother-in-law empty-handed.'" Then Naomi
said, "Wait, my daughter, until you find out what
happens. For the man will not rest until the
matter is settled today."*

Single anointed women are very strong willed.
They are independent, they take care of our
business and are ready to claim the victory. That is
great, but when it comes to being found, and being
a wife; your job is to submit. Submission is the act
of taking all that you are in your anointing, your
gifts, and your talents, and placing them under
your husband for him to cover you properly. You
must let your husband lead and what better place
to practice following but in courting.

Boaz instructed Ruth to lie at his feet until
morning. In the morning, he sent her home with
food and her mother-in-law, her confidant, wanted
an update. Ruth told Naomi everything.
Remember, Naomi was her safe place, so she told
her everything that took place on the threshing
floor. Naomi continues to advise telling Ruth to
relax, wait and let him do the rest! Ladies, if you
don't allow him to lead as your "intended," you will

have issues allowing him to lead as your husband, and you will be totally out of order.

In your courting and into your marriage, your Boaz wants to rescue you. He wants to be your hero, your Superman, but he can't do his job if you don't allow him. Naomi's wisdom—wait—and I say that to you. Wait for him to bring the ring, wait for him to propose, wait for him to show love to you first so that the order of things set in your singleness will continue into marriage. You never want your anxiety or excitement of being found to ruin things; a sober woman is a successful woman.

While your Boaz is preparing things for your future, stay submitted to your spiritual covering, continue to walk in purpose and do what God has instructed you to do. Allow him to put things in place. Permit him to live up to the covenant words in which he promised you. Allow him to lead so you can be in order and follow.

CHAPTER 4

Will He Assume The Responsibility of You?

Ruth 4: 1-6 (GW) Boaz went to the city gate and sat there. Just then, the relative about whom he had spoken was passing by. Boaz said, "Please come over here and sit, my friend." So the man came over and sat down. Then Boaz chose ten men who were leaders of that city and said, "Sit here." So they also sat down. Boaz said to the man, "Naomi, who has come back from the country of Moab, is selling the field that belonged to our relative Elimelech. So I said that I would inform you. Buy it in the presence of these men sitting here and in the presence of the leaders of our people. If you wish to buy back the property, you can buy back the property. But if you do not wish to buy back the property, tell me. Then I will know that I am next in line because there is no other relative except me." The man said, "I'll buy back the property." Boaz continued, "When you buy the field from Naomi, you will also assume responsibility for the Moabite Ruth, the dead man's widow. This keeps the inheritance in the dead man's name." The man replied, "In that case I cannot assume responsibility for her. If I did, I would ruin my inheritance. Take all my rights to buy back the property for yourself, because I cannot assume that responsibility."

Before we get into the last chapter of Ruth, let's pause for a second and discuss the word "wait". The obvious definition of the word wait is "to remain inactive or in a state of repose, as until something expected happens (often followed by for, till, or until)." However, I would like to offer a different perspective to that word as many single women will announce they are "waiting" to be found. We are accustomed to seeing this definition in operation but never really apply it to the single season.

When you go into a restaurant, a waiter comes to your table to take your order, delivers your drinks, your food, brings you a fork if you drop yours, brings you dessert, brings you your check for payment, goes in the back runs your credit card and then brings the receipt back to you. While you are in the restaurant the only one doing the real work is the WAITER!

I believe that in your single state you should be waiting (serving or attending to) your God-given purpose in a great way. If God has called you to assist the homeless, you should be hosting food drives, clothing drives, soliciting for funds to help support those in need financially; you should be working! This is not the season for you to be sitting down, wallowing, complaining and declaring you're bored, but it is the time for you to be actively working the threshing floor assigned for your life. This is the most opportune time for you to work in the greatest capacity of ministry, business, and community activism, etc. remaining focused on the individual vision for your life. Once you are married you are still to walk in the purpose given to you by God before the foundation of the world but your purpose and your husband's purpose now become one, and you must do what is necessary first and foremost to HELP him with the vision God has given to your family as whole.

Single women who say that have nothing to do because they aren't married are using their marital status as a lame excuse. Do you know how many people need your help, need assistance in getting a prayer through, how many people are waiting on you to write your book, start your business and could careless if you have a husband or not. They just need your gifts operating in the earth.

In this season you're not waiting on the man but you're in a waiting season, serving the Lord as a single individual. Paul said in I Corinthians 7:1, Now, concerning the things that you wrote about:

It's good for men not to get married, yet he knew that singleness was not everyone's lot in life, that is why he also taught on the husbands and wives responsibility in the home. During this season your body is not your husband's because you don't have one, your time schedule is not built around someone else you have the ability and the freedom to move about and do some awesome things. Jesus and Paul were more successful singles because they walked in purpose and stayed focused on their duty to God, They walked in authority and were obedient to the Holy Spirit. This is the proper way to wait in your single season.

Now back to Ruth and Boaz.

Boaz was a man of integrity, business and excellence; He was not perfect. God's daughters should desire a man with vision, a man who knows how to strategize, a man with wisdom, love, patience and compassion. You may have never seen a natural example of a man like this, but that doesn't mean he doesn't exist. We are to be people of God, walking by faith and not by sight, and if God gives us the desires of our heart, it's time for you to raise the bar! You should desire God's best and not settle for a man just to say you are married. When you raise your bar, you will ask more important question than what high school he attended. You will inquire about his goals, his aspirations, what has God given him to do that you will have to help him accomplish?

Now I don't believe everyone knows their complete purpose in God but this man who wants to be your husband must be aware of his foundational vision for his life, which is who and what God has called him to be and do. You should never want to waste your time with someone who cannot see spiritually. He will be leading you, and if he can't see now he's going to lead you right over that spiritual or natural cliff.

In the first six verses of the last chapter of Ruth, Boaz is ready to seal the deal. However, because he is a man of his word and a man of honesty and integrity, he must follow the law of the land and present an opportunity to the one who is next in line. Boaz informs this relative that he and Naomi, Elimelech's widow, are selling the field they owned, and by law he has first right to buy it. Now the relative is excited and ready to sign on the dotted line until Boaz informs him what else comes with the land. Verse 5 reads Boaz continued, "When you buy the field from Naomi, you will also assume responsibility for the Moabite

Ruth, the dead man's widow. This keeps the inheritance in the dead man's name." Whoa nelly!! The relative is not ready for the additional obligation of a dead man's widow. He kindly declines and states he cannot assume responsibility for Ruth.

This scenario in these first verses is indicative of most single women's lives who have been left at the altar, left holding the bag and left feeling rejected. Yet again we must change our perspective in regards to be "rejected". The one who had every right to marry Ruth, made one simple yet profound statement, "I cannot assume this responsibility." You may have dated/courted a man or men whom you believed was "the one", but he could not assume the responsibility for you. Not who you were then, but who you would become. He wasn't graced to cover you and love you like Christ loved the church. Neither was he anointed to encourage you in your purpose or support you in your endeavors. He was ready to take ownership of what was below your waist, but not full responsibility of your purpose, your destiny, your accomplishments, business or ministry. He was not equipped to assume the role of being your hero or your husband! Therefore, there is no need for you to be in a "woe is me" state if he walked away.

He wasn't the one to be accountable for your restoration, your recompense or your success! The relative is being honest, "I don't want to mess up my inheritance concerning something for which I don't want to be responsible." As a result, he handed his rights over to Boaz.

PASS THE SHOE

Ruth 4: 7-11 (GW) (This is the way it used to be in Israel concerning buying back property and exchanging goods: In order to make every matter legal, a man would take off his sandal and give it to the other man. This was the way a contract was publicly approved in Israel.) So when the man said to Boaz, "Buy it for yourself," he took off his sandal. Then Boaz said to the leaders and to all the people, "Today you are witnesses that I have bought from Naomi all that belonged to Elimelech and all that belonged to Chilion and Mahlon. In addition, I have bought as my wife the Moabite Ruth, Mahlon's widow, to keep the inheritance in the dead man's name. In this way the dead man's name will not be cut off from his relatives or from the public records. Today you are witnesses." All the people who were at the gate, including the leaders, said, "We are witnesses. May the Lord make this wife, who is coming into your home, like Rachel and Leah, both of whom built our family of Israel. So show your strength of character in Ephrathah and make a name for yourself in Bethlehem. Also, from the descendant whom the Lord will give you from this young woman, may your family become like the family of Perez, the son whom Tamar gave birth to for Judah."

Boaz was in love with Ruth. What he promised her he fulfilled. He wanted to give her everything, and he wanted to give her a better life. A good husband-to-be knows that his life is no longer important for his desires become what his wife desires, and he loves her like Christ loves the church, and Christ died for the church.

An awesome question to ask a man proposing marriage to you is, "are you ready to be responsible and accountable for my success?" If they aren't, stay right under God's cloak until He reveals you to the one who will become insignificant so that you may be significant.

When C. Kevin Ford found me, he showed me very early on that he supported everything God had put in my heart to do. He attended my conferences, he kept the children when I had to preach, he supported me in business, and there were never signs of jealousy or envy, because we are one, and my success is only because he covers me well!

Boaz announces to everyone in the market that he will purchase the land and assume responsibility for Ruth. Notice his class and sophistication; he makes a pubic announcement of his intentions! Ladies, beware of men who hide you or hide that they are in a relationship with you. They are NO good! Now I don't agree with your relationship having to be on pubic display through Facebook and twitter, however, when you don't know those closest to him and he doesn't want you to, *Houston, we have a problem.* Men who hide you are bad news; they don't know your worth, they don't understand your value, and if he shows off his car more than he does you, he needs to hit the road. Secrecy and isolation are sure signs that he's not the one because what he does before marriage, he will do in marriage as well. You don't have to be paranoid, but you do have to be wise.

Boaz honored Ruth buy doing IT right! He didn't take advantage of her physically, he didn't demand anything from her to marry him, and he made a public announcement in following through with his promise to her, "But if he does not wish to take care of you, then, I solemnly swear, as the Lord lives, I will take care of you myself." Boaz was serious about his word to her and took it upon himself to handle the legal transaction. He covered her throughout the entire process. I don't know about you but when I see my man handling the business, that is sexy to me, and it makes a woman feel protected!

THE FRUIT OF YOUR MARRIAGE

Ruth 4:13-15 (GW) Then Boaz took Ruth home, and she became his wife. He slept with her, and the Lord gave her the ability to become pregnant. So she gave birth to a son. The women said to Naomi, "Praise the Lord, who has remembered today to give you someone who will take care of you. The child's name will be famous in Israel. He will bring you a new life and support you in your old age. Your daughter-in-law who loves you is better to you than seven sons, because she has given birth." Naomi took the child, held him on her lap, and became his guardian. The women in the neighborhood said, "Naomi has a son." So they gave him the name Obed. He became the father of Jesse, who was the father of David.

Pastor Myles Munroe is often known to say that if the purpose of something is unknown abuse is inevitable. There is an enormous amount of divorce in the world and especially in the church. Why? Because many do not know the purpose of marriage so the result is abuse of this covenant institution. Extra marital affairs, verbal and physical abuse and divorce is inevitable when as a whole we have not been taught the purpose of marriage. Marriage is not a safe haven for single folks to have legal sex. It's not a place for folks who have had children together out of wedlock to choose to live simply because they have procreated. Marriage is not a reason to be married.

God's purpose for marriage from the beginning was, Genesis 1:26-28 (NIV) Then God said, "Let us make mankind in our image, in our likeness, so that they may rule over the fish in the sea and the birds in the sky, over the livestock and all the wild animals, and over all the creatures that move along the ground." So God created mankind in his own image, in the image of God he created the male and female he created them. God blessed them and said to them, "Be fruitful and increase in number; fill the earth and subdue it. Rule over the fish in the sea and the birds in the sky and over every living creature that moves on the ground."

Marriage was made to bring forth fruit! The Lord instructed male and female to be fruitful and increase in number to fill the earth and subdue it (have dominion). This was humanity's charge so God created the institution of marriage in order for this to be fulfilled. Adam and Eve were to produce naturally and spiritually. Your marriage is bigger than you and your husband. It's about what your marriage is destined to produce. It is to bring forth businesses, ministries, books, children, positive change in the community and positive change in your families. The FRUIT of your marriage is to be generational and legacy driven!

Boaz and Ruth came together as two least likely. Ruth was a Moabite, the enemy of the Israelites. Boaz had no legal claim to buy the land or rightfully marry Ruth. Nonetheless, God's plan for their lives was for them to be married and be the ancestors of the Messiah. Their union produced Obed who was David's grandfather. Boaz and Ruth's names are listed in the genealogy of Jesus in Matthew chapter one. Through this union Naomi was even restored as Ruth brought forth a son. Remember marriage is God's idea, and as He has ordained marriage for your life. Your union should bring forth fruit that will restore people to God, people desiring to be married and cause your legacy in the earth to be documented by man.

CHAPTER 5

Conclusion

*He who finds a wife finds what is good and
receives favor from the Lord.*
Proverbs 18:22 (NIV)

*Houses and wealth are inherited from parents,
but a prudent wife is from the Lord.*
Proverbs 19:14 (NIV)

*"Who can find a wife with a strong character?
She is worth far more than jewels.*
Proverbs 31:10 (GW)

MY LAST WORDS...

I cannot express enough that in this season of your life you must renew your mind and change your perspective in regards to how you view your singleness. It's time to stop thinking of your singleness as a crutch and think of it as a trampoline, a vehicle that will catapult you into the next phase of your life. However, if you don't get on the trampoline and start jumping it doesn't work; it's just a big piece of equipment sitting in your backyard collecting dust. You have to play your part to be a successful, saved, single individual.

This is the time for you to become intimate with God. Remember, "Life HAPPENS!" and sometimes it causes us to devalue ourselves, but during your intimate times with God He will restore you, build you back up, and heal you from the crown of your head to the soles of your feet and make you secure in who He has made you to be. In your single life you must spend time with God.

In 1999, I received prophetic instructions that God wanted me to spend more times of intimacy with Him. In these times of intimacy He was going to love on me. I was going to love on Him, and He was going to show me who I was in Him. God reassured me that the purpose for these times of intimacy was to get me prepared for marriage. As I was intimate with Him in the spirit, my husband would love me just the same in the natural. That was seven years before I met my husband. Now trust me I did not stick to my end of the bargain, and I strayed from my place at His feet, but when I got back on track, I would have wonderful times of prayer and fasting with God, I was in my word day and night, and I began to understand the true meaning of unconditional love. I believe it was when my time of intimacy with God began to peak that I knew my husband was getting closer.

My spirit would cry in prayer to God and in conversation with my family that I was ready to submit, not ready for a wedding, not ready for a honeymoon, not even ready to get married, but I was ready to submit to my husband. The Lord was letting me know that I was now ready to experience this same level of natural intimacy with my husband that I had experienced spiritually with Him.

During times of intimacy, God will love you from the inside out. This is the place where you will be cultivated, preserved and kept under the cloak. This is the place where you will be taught how to serve God, love God, and submit to God, and when it peaks it's time for you to enter marriage. That same submission, intimacy, that same love is then unto your husband. It's in the intimate place that you feel secure.

How intimate are you now with the Lord? How much time do you spend with God, just you and him, not when you run to church for intercessory prayer or choir rehearsal but just "you and God" time? Is it consistent or infrequent? Is it a time that you value or is it rushed? How you are with God in your times of intimacy you will be with your husband. Your husband is not really going to like you much if all you do is come to him when the bills are due. No time of conversation, you're not kicking it with him when he wants to watch the basketball game or you're not trying to find out what makes him happy. No man wants to be married to a woman like that. Intimacy is a necessity in marriage and it is in your single season with God that you will learn how to be an effective partner.

As well, remember there is no fear in spending time with God. I reiterate, if you're courting or dating someone and most of the time you are afraid of them, or you're dating someone and you're arguing and fighting, and there is no peace, you know you don't do that with God, so why would you continue in that type of relationship?

In due season you will be unveiled to your husband. Through discernment God will show him who you are and the vision God has for your life. God will show him the love and compassion that you have for others or that you walk strongly in administrative skills, or that you are a Prophet, Evangelist or an Entrepreneur. The Lord will unveil these things to your husband as he discerns that you are his wife. In the meantime please do not pull off the cloak God has placed over you to protect you from counterfeits. When you are ready, when God has healed you and delivered you from past hurt and matured you in your faith in Him, then He will reveal you properly to your husband.

Ladies you are valuable to God and he will not unveil or reveal you to someone who will devalue you or abuse your worth. That's generally your flesh that wants to be revealed to the wrong one. Yet God wants to disclose you to the one who will love you like Christ loves the church, and He's not going to throw His pearls to swine. So stay, wait, be totally restored, let God heal you, let Him take away the dirt and grime of life that has made you seem un-valuable, even though you aren't.

This presentation will be likened to the unveiling of a fine piece of art such as the Mona Lisa, the Sistine Chapel or equivalent to when God brought Eve to Adam and her beauty wowed him.

God knows the day of your revelation, just like He knew Ruth's. Are you willing to wait for Revelation Day?

ABOUT THE AUTHOR

Candace N. Ford is an
entrepreneur, author,
speaker, an ordained
minister and spiritual
strategist, who believes in
producing multiple
streams of income. She is
the CEO of Love Clones
Publishing, a full service
publishing firm and
together with her
husband Kevin Ford, the apostolic overseer
of Abiding Presence International Alliance.

Graduating from DePaul University with a
Bachelors of Science degree in Accountancy, she
began work at PricewaterhouseCoopers, LLP as a
financial auditor. Her accounting career continued
with positions at various companies such as Sara
Lee Corporation, Solomon Edwards Consulting
and United Airlines. While working in the
accounting field, she believed there was more for
her to do to assist others, not financially, but

spiritually. She began her first ministry to women in 2005.

Through her ministry, CNF Ministries, Candace is dedicated to helping men and women of God acknowledge and develop their gifts and talents in the earth. Through teaching and one-on-one mentoring she endeavors to cultivate kingdom leaders as they recognize their uniqueness in the marketplace or ministry while motivating them to maximize their leadership potential.

Candace and her husband live in Dallas, TX, with their son Nicholas and daughters, Brianna and Madison.

Other Books written by Candace N. Ford
Committed 2 Commune
The 180° Revolution
Colors of My Walk
Declarations of the Kingdom Driven Entrepreneur
The Answer Key

Connect with Candace N. Ford:
Website: www.cnfministries.com
Facebook: @ford.candace
Twitter: @fordcandace